# Joe Cocker Adult Coloring Book

**British Knight and Pop Rock Legend, Gritty Vocalist and Dancer Inspired Adult Coloring Book**

**Natali Harris**

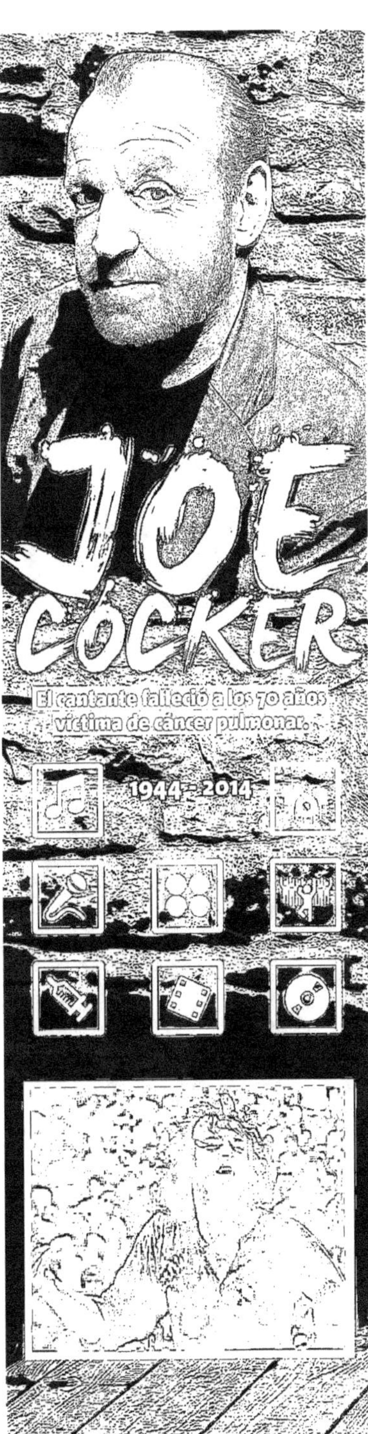

JOE
COCKER
El cantante falleció a los 70 años
víctima de cáncer pulmonar.
1944 - 2014

Joe
Cocker
Live

Joe Cocker
1944-2014

HEAR 4 TRACK STEREO SOUND
SEE MULTIPLE SCREEN IMAGES
MAD DOGS & ENGLISHMEN
STARRING
JOE COCKER
the notorious and his 2 member immoral piano co.
LEON RUSSELL
the master
of space & time
see them perform in the pleasure palaces of America

JOE COCKER
THE ESSENTIAL COLLECTION
THE LEGEND
including WITH A LITTLE HELP FROM MY FRIENDS • DELTA LADY
UP WHERE WE BELONG • THE LETTER • YOU ARE SO BEAUTIFUL

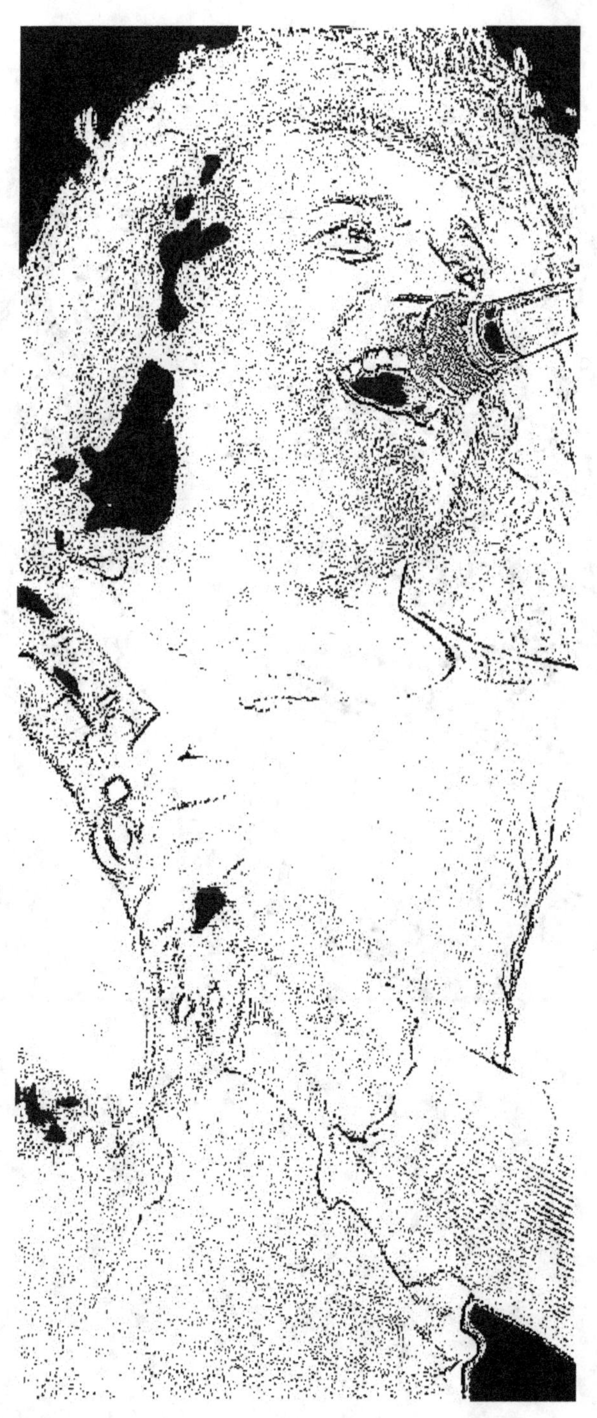

1/10 artist proof   "Cochumil"

I get by
with a little help
from my friends...
-Joe Cocker

THE
EN'S CO      TS
BUCKINGHA
Produced
B B
FREE
WINONA

COCKER HAPPY

# Joe Cocker
### POPPPND

ROCK PARTY
ROCK PARTY

the best of JOE
cocker

STATES

BRAVO-Porträt
Joe Cocker

www.ingramcontent.com/pod-product-compliance
Lightning Source LLC
Chambersburg PA
CBHW051927250726

48659CB00002B/888